The Lucky Star

The Lucky Star

Charles H. Brookfield,
Ivan Caryll and
Helen Lenoir

MINT EDITIONS

The Lucky Star was first published in 1899.

This edition published by Mint Editions 2021.

ISBN 9781513281469 | E-ISBN 9781513286488

Published by Mint Editions®

**MINT
EDITIONS**

minteditionbooks.com

Publishing Director: Jennifer Newens
Design & Production: Rachel Lopez Metzger
Project Manager: Micaela Clark
Typesetting: Westchester Publishing Services

Dramatis Personæ

King Ouf the First	Mr. Walter Passmore
The Baron Tabasco (*Ambassador-Extraordinary from King Mataquin*)	Mr. Henry A. Lytton
Siroco (*the Astrologer Royal*)	Mr. Fred Wright, Jun.
Tapioca (*Private Secretary to Baron Tabasco*)	Mr. Robert Evett
Cancan (*a Citizen*)	Mr. Leonard Russell
Princess Laoula (*Daughter of King Mataquin*)	Miss Ruth Vincent
Aloës (*Daughter of Tabasco and Lady-in-Waiting to the Princess*)	Miss Isabel Jay
Maids of Honour:	
Oasis	Miss Jessie Rose
Asphodel	Miss Madge Moyse
Zinnia	Miss Mildred Baker
Adza (*the Court Dancer*)	Miss Katie Vesey
Lazuli (*a Travelling Painter*)	Miss Emmie Owen

Citizens, Guards, Courtiers, and Ladies-in-Waiting.

Act I.—A Public Square (*T.E. Ryan*)
Act II —Throne Room in the King's Palace (*W. Harford*)
Act III.—A Summer-Room in the Palace (*W. Harford*)

Produced under the stage direction of Mr. R. Barker
Musical Director, Mr. François Cellier

The costumes designed by Mr. Percy Anderson, and executed by Miss Fisher, Messrs. B.J. Simmons and Co., and Madame Léon. The properties by Mr. Edward Siedle, of New York, and Mr. Skelly, of London. Stage Machinist, Mr. P. White. Electrician, Mr. Lyons. Stage Manager, Mr. W.H. Seymour. Acting Manager, Mr. J.W. Beckwith. The dances by Mr. W. Warde (*by kind permission of Mr. George Edwards*)

Act I

Scene.—*A public square R.I.E. Set observatory with practicable balcony on which mounted telescope stands. Front profile of observatory only on the stage. Sign over door, reading, "Siroco, Astronomer Royal. Your fortune told while you wait." L.I.E. profile front of Inn. Sign of a red dragon over door. Practicable balcony to Inn also. Set tree R.C. banked up with grass mats. Profile houses R. and L.H. Back drop landscape with water effect. At rise of curtain day is just breaking, and as the scene progresses sunrise effect and change to broad daylight. Citizens are discovered.*

Chorus.
(words by Adrian Ross)

Men: Night is done, but it is not day,
    Only a twilight, quiet and grey,
    Brightening slowly, far away—
        Far away.
    Light winds rustle in the bough and brake,
    Little ripples run up the lake—
    Waken, day of May, awake!
        Now awake!
(Sunrise effect, girls coming in bearing garlands and baskets of flowers)
Girls: Spring's in the air,
        Winter is ended;
            Blossoms unclose,
            Golden and rose!
        Blossoms we bear,
            Scented and splendid,
                Worthy to bring
                Unto our King!
All: Hail to the day
        Festal and famous,
            Day when he smiled
            First as a child!
        Loyalty may
            Rightly inflame us,
                Bidding us sing,

"Hail to our King!"

Cancan enters L., from Inn.

CANCAN: Now the king that we are under, with a fal la la!
   With a skill at which we wonder, with a fal la la!
      Has provided recreation for the yearly jubilation,
ALL: Singing fal lal, fal lal, lirra lirra lay!
CANCAN: There are conjuror and tumbler, with a fal la la!
   And some actors for the humbler, with a fal la la!
      But the special institution is the yearly execution,
ALL: With a fal lal, fal lal, lirra lirra lay!
CANCAN: So we celebrate the season of the year,
   When our monarch condescended to appear,
      Gaily voicing our rejoicing
      Thus, in thorough-going thunderous cheer!
ALL: So we celebrate the season of the year, etc.
CANCAN: There are fountains fair and cunning, with a fal la la!
   In a rosy rillet running, with a fal la la!
      Where the poet from the garret quaffs a thinner dinner
      claret,
ALL: Singing fal lal, fal lal, lirra lirra lay!
CANCAN: There are gardens and pavilions, with a fal la la!
   Lit with fairy lamps in millions, with a fal la la!
      And we drain the public pockets for illimitable rockets,
ALL: Singing fal lal, fal lal, lirra lirra lay!
CANCAN: So we give three hips succeeded by "Hooray!"
   For the monarch whom we cheerfully obey;
      Praise him proudly, laud him loudly,
   Wishing him numberless returns of the day!
ALL: So we give three hips succeeded by "Hooray!" etc.

DANCE.

(*After which exeunt all R. and L. Kedas has entered L.U.E. at commencement
of dance. He wears a long cloak and slouch hat, like a conspirator*)
KEDAS: It's no use! I've spent the entire night trying to coax a
   treasonable speech or act out of some one, and failed completely.
   But a victim for His Majesty's annual fête must be had; and as,
   by our laws, treason is the only crime punishable by death, some
   one must be incited to commit treason. (*Siroco appears on balcony*

of observatory R.H) Ah! there's Siroco! Perhaps he can give me an astral tip. (*Calling*) Hi, there! Siroco!

SIROCO: What can I do for His Majesty's Minister of Police?

KEDAS: You can do a great deal for me, if you will.

SIROCO: How?

KEDAS: By uttering a few treasonable sentiments. I'm not particular. Revile the memory of the King's grandmother, or curse the income-tax. Anything will do.

SIROCO: What should I do that for?

KEDAS: To enable me to arrest you, of course. Don't you know that to-day is His Majesty's fête day, and that for seventeen years he has celebrated it by publicly executing some one, by a novel death method, annually invented by himself.

SIROCO: Certainly.

KEDAS: As Minister of Police he looks to me to provide the victim.

SIROCO: Come into the house, and I'll cast your horoscope for you. The stars may extricate you from your trouble. (*Exit from balcony*)

KEDAS: I hope they'll be lively about it. (*Exit into house R.I.E. Enter mysteriously R.B.C. Tabasco, Tapioca, Laoula, and Aloës. All are in travelling costume, Tapioca, laden with all the impedimenta of a travelling party, struggles on last, nearly concealed by the articles he carries. He lets them fall with a crash. All four come down stage mysteriously*)

QUARTET.—LAOULA, ALOËS, TABASCO, and TAPIOCA.
(words by Adrian Ross)

ALL: Hush! hark! is anyone near?
    Hist! ha! can anyone hear?
    Hi! ho! does anyone see?
    Nobody know who we may be!

TABASCO: I am the Plenipotentiary,

ALOËS: I am the great ambassadress!

TAPIOCA: I am their private secretary,

LAOULA: I am a fair Princess!

ALL: But none the mystery may unravel,
    Why thus in popular garb we go;

LAOULA: There are reasons why we travel
    In a strict incognito!

And I—

ALOËS: Would die—

TABASCO: Before I own, by word unwary,
   I am the Plenipotentiary!

ALL: We are incognito.

All produce commercial travellers' bags of samples.

   Take our bits of baggage and rummage 'em,
   Toss them to and fro;
   Look in mine and his and hers,
   We're commercial travellers!
   All our goods are genuine Brummagem,
      Marked with prices low—
   That is how we manage to journey incognito!

   He is the Plenipotentiary, etc.
   Incognito!

TABASCO: Tapioca!

TAPIOCA: Yes, Excellency.

TABASCO: Is all the luggage there?

TAPIOCA: Fourteen pieces, your Excellency.

TABASCO: Fourteen? (*Angrily*) Miserable dolt that you are! There should be fifteen! What have you done with the other one, idiot?

ALOËS: You forget, Papa, No. 15 was the lunch, and we ate it on the way.

TABASCO: Then some one should have told me so. (*Exit Tapioca R.*) Another thing. How many times must I tell you not to call me "Papa"?

ALOËS: But you are!

TABASCO: By the laws of nature, I am. But by the requirements of diplomacy, I am nothing of the sort. Diplomatically you care the Princess Laoula, and the Princess here (*indicating Laoula*) is my wife.

LAOULA: Diplomatically only.

TABASCO: Of course. Such ruses constitute the subtle art of diplomacy. It would be perfectly easy, for instance, for me to proclaim to every one, "I am the Baron Tabasco—King Mataquin's special envoy and plenipotentiary. This is my daughter, Aloës—this is my private secretary, Tapioca."

TAPIOCA: Yes, sir.

TABASCO: Don't interrupt! "This young lady is the peerless Princess Laoula." I could easily say all that. Nine asses out of ten would have said all that.

ALOËS: It would have saved a lot of complication.

TABASCO: Precisely. That's why I didn't say it. The day when politics are conducted straightforwardly and without circumlocution will be a cold day for ministers and office-holders.

ALOËS: But a sunny day for everybody else!

LAOULA: But why is all this make-believe necessary? Why must we conceal our proper rank, disguise ourselves as tradespeople, and travel on foot like this?

TABASCO: Because it's diplomatic.

ALOËS (*to Laoula*): I feel as if we were children again, playing with dolls.

LAOULA: I almost wish we were. We were happier then!

BALLAD.—LAOULA.
(adapted from the American version
by Aubrey Hopwood)

When I was a child of three,
    Heigh ho! Long ago!
Happy as a child could be,
    Heigh ho! Long ago!
I'd a little doll, whose eyes
Shone as blue as summer skies;
Though she never spoke a word,
Yet I quite believe she heard
Every childish hope and fear
That I whispered in her ear;
All my griefs to her I told,
In those nursery days of old;
When I was a child of three,
    Heigh ho! Long ago!

Even as the years went by,
    Heigh ho! Long ago!
Faithful to my doll was I,
    Heigh ho! Long ago!

Time has dulled her eyes of blue—
Rosy cheeks have lost their hue,
Shabby was her dainty dress—
Yet I loved her none the less;
For to me it always seemed
That she dreamed the dreams I dreamed,
And the secrets that I told
As in nursery days of old,
When I was a child of three,
    Heigh ho! Long ago!

Childish toys are thrown away,
    Heigh ho! Long ago!
I have grown too old for play,
    Heigh ho! Long ago!
Friends I have, both old and new,
Some are false and some are true;
Some who praise and some who blame,
None who's ever quite the same
As the friend I can't forget,
As the doll I still regret,
When my foolish fancy strays,
To the dear old nursery days,
When I was a child of three,
    Heigh ho! Long ago!

TAPIOCA (*re-entering, aside*): He's a cheerful diplomat!

TABASCO (*to Tapioca*): What was that? (*Angrily*) What do you mean by mumbling? Don't you know that as my private secretary your first duty is to hold your tongue?

TAPIOCA: Oh, come, I say! I've stood quite enough of this. I resign.

ALOËS (*running to Tapioca*): No! No! Don't do that!

TAPIOCA (*to Aloës, who is in dumb show trying to soothe him. Laoula at the same time is arguing with Tabasco*): I can't help it. Do you think I've got cast-iron sensibilities?

ALOËS (*to Tapioca*): But for my sake, darling!

TAPIOCA (*to Aloës*): Look out! He'll see us. All right, I'll try it once more.

ALOËS (*to Tabasco*): He withdraws his resignation. So there!

TABASCO (*aside*): That's the ninth time he's resigned in a week.
    (*Aloud*) I'll overlook your offence this time, young man. But be

careful! For some of these days I shall lose my temper. I warn you! (*Looking round him*) Here's a decent- looking inn. We had better go in and tidy ourselves. (*Offers an arm to Laoula*) Tapioca! Bring my daughter and the luggage. (*Repetition of Quartet. All exeunt mysteriously into inn L.H.; Tapioca last with luggage. When all are off Lazuli enters, dressed as a wandering painter, with easel, etc*)

LAZULI (*looking anxiously round*): No. I've missed them! Lost all trace of them! Well, it doesn't really matter. I couldn't have spoken to her. I know what I will do, I'll make a sketch of her sweet face while it's fresh in my memory. (*Erects his easel, spreads out his painting materials, and begins to paint*) I wonder who they were? The men were commonplace enough. But the women! One was pretty, but the other was an angel! I had but a glimpse of her sweet face. She has vanished from my life, but she shall never leave my heart. (*Goes on painting. Siroco and Kedas enter from house R.I.E.*)

SIROCO: I hope you're satisfied?

KEDAS: Satisfied? I am simply surfeited with content. The stars promise a victim within an hour. My reputation as Minister of Police is saved. Siroco, I am your debtor for life. (*Shakes Siroco's hand warmly and exit hastily L.H.*)

SIROCO: Debtor for life, eh? Well, if all my customers did business on that basis, where should I be?

LAZULI (*who has overheard last speeches, aside*): A fortune- teller! I wonder if he would reveal my idol's whereabouts! (*To Siroco*) You cast horoscopes, don't you?

SIROCO: Occasionally.

LAZULI: All right. Cast mine. (*Extending hand*) How's that for a hand?

SIROCO: It's like most hands I hold nowadays—not filled.

LAZULI: Oh, I see! (*Produces coin and extends hand again with coin displayed*) How's that? Better?

SIROCO (*pocketing coin*): Decidedly so. (*Aside*) He's the first cast customer I've had in a fortnight. (*To Lazuli*) Remain here, young man, until I've prepared a chart.

LAZULI: I suppose your horoscopes are reliable?

SIROCO: Reliable! Young man, rather than tell an untruth I have lost customers innumerable. I will give you an instance or two:

Song.—Siroco.

Once a lady came to me, she was stout as stout could be,
 And her age was the uncertain kind of age;
She considered acting nice, and upon her friends' advice,
 Well, she really thought of going on the stage!
Did I think she'd win success? Well, I tried to answer "yes,"
 But my conscience wouldn't bear the heavy strain;
It was awkward, but, forsooth, I was forced to tell the truth,
 And she'll never want a horoscope again!
 No, she'll never want a horoscope again!
 From eclipsing Sarah Bernhardt she'll refrain;
When the stars revealed her age, she retired in a rage, And she'll
 never want a horoscope again!

BOTH: No, she'll never want a horoscope again, etc.

SIROCO: From the Transvaal, one fine day, I'd a client come my way,
 And he wore a patriarchal sort of beard;
He's a most tenacious clutch, and he spoke in double-Dutch,
 And a rather Boerish person he appeared!
He inquired if I thought that the armaments he bought
 Over Britain an advantage would obtain?
It was awkward, but, forsooth, I was forced to tell the truth,
 And he'll never want a horoscope again!
 No, he'll never want a horoscope again!
 He has purchased all those armaments in vain;
I just mentioned "Doctor Jim," and that seemed enough
 to him,
 And he'll never want a horoscope again!

BOTH: No, he'll never want a horoscope again, etc.

SIROCO: Once a party called on me, he was good as good could be,
 You could tell that by his black and glossy clo'es!
Then he wore a white cravat and a "go-to-meeting" hat,
 And he murmured moral maxims through his nose!
Well, he told me, with a frown, we'd put Sunday music down,
 Did I think that all his efforts would be vain?
It was awkward, but, forsooth, I was forced to tell the truth,
 And he'll never want a horoscope again!
 No, he'll never want a horoscope again!
 When I told him all his efforts were in vain,

Well, he gave the door a slam and I think he murmured—Tut!
    So he'll never want a horoscope again!
BOTH: So he'll never want a horoscope again, etc.
SIROCO: Now one day I met a man and he came from the Soudan,
    And he called himself a Mahdi, I believe;
He's a wicked-looking eye, seemed the kind of man who'd try
    To conceal the ace of trumps within his sleeve!
Well, he called on me to learn if his luck would ever turn,
    If a victory once more he would obtain?
It was awkward, but, forsooth, I was forced to tell the truth,
    And he'll never want a horoscope again!
    No, he'll never want a horoscope again!
    He may struggle, but he'll struggle on in vain,
There's a Kitchener in use that will cook his little goose:
    And he'll never want a horoscope again! Both. And he'll never
    want a horoscope again, etc.

Exit Siroco hastily into house R.I.E.

LAZULI: What a fool I am! I've given him the last coin I had in the
world, and haven't had my breakfast! Never mind—they say that
a sound sleep is as good as a dinner! I'll try it, anyway. I wonder
what the stars will have to say to me? (*Lazuli lies down on bank B.C.,
and falls asleep. Tabasco and Tapioca enter from inn L.I.E.*) Tabasco.
And now for the King! Tapioca!

TAPIOCA: Your Excellency?

TABASCO: You will accompany me at a respectful distance.

TAPIOCA: But the ladies, your Excellency—

TABASCO: The ladies? It isn't a question of ladies. It's a question of
diplomacy. I am the bearer of an ultimatum.

TAPIOCA: What's that?

TABASCO: You'll know soon enough, and so will the King. Now then,
for the Palace! (*Exit L.3.E. followed by Tapioca. Aloës appears at door
of inn, as if spying to see if the coast is clear. When Tabasco and Tapioca
are off, Aloës comes down from the inn and calls back*)

ALOËS: Come along, Princess! They're gone.

LAOULA (*appearing at inn door, L.I.E.*): But he told us to stay in our
room.

ALOËS: Who? Papa? I know he did; but you know diplomats never
mean what they say.

LAOULA: I'm afraid!

ALOËS (*going to Laoula*): Afraid of what, you goose? (*Half pushes, half pulls Laoula from inn to C.*) Do you think any one is going to eat you? (*As she releases Laoula, the latter discovers Lazuli*)

LAOULA: Great heavens! (*Clings to Aloës*)

ALOËS (*also startled*): What is it? Oh dear, what is it?

LAOULA: It's—it's a man!

ALOËS: Is that all? I thought it was a mouse, or a caterpillar. Where is he?

LAOULA (*pointing out Lazuli*): There!

ALOËS (*looking at him*): So he is—and asleep. Rather a good-looking young man, too.

LAOULA: Extremely good-looking.

ALOËS: I feel as if I had seen him somewhere before.

LAOULA: Of course we have seen him before. It's the young man whom we passed just now on the road.

ALOËS: So it is. What a memory you have for faces! (*Examining easel*) He's an artist. Look! I believe he was painting your portrait!

LAOULA (*looking at picture*): Was he? How sweet of him!

ALOËS: He soon got tired of it, though. (*Approaches Lazuli and looks at him*)

LAOULA: Come away quickly! He might wake up.

ALOËS: I know it. For fear he might not, though, I'm going to assist him. (*Pulls some long straws or blades of grass from bank*)

LAOULA: Aloës! Be careful! What are you going to do?

ALOËS: Wait a minute and you'll see. (*Aloës begins to tickle Lazuli gently with a straw. He suddenly jumps up and catches each girl round the waist*)

LAZULI (*to Laoula*): I've caught you at last! Now then, who are you?

LAOULA: I—I don't know.

LAZULI: Don't know?

ALOËS (*coming to her rescue*): We're in business. We're from Swanbill and Headgear's.

LAOULA: We're travelling for the firm.

LAZULI: Who were those two men with you?

ALOËS: They were gentleman from behind the counter.

LAOULA: From Swanbill and Headgear's. They're travelling for the firm too.

LAZULI: That's all right. (*To Laoula*) What's your name?

LAOULA: Laoula.

LAZULI: Laoula, I love you with my whole being.

LAOULA: Already?

ALOËS: Well, you don't lose much time, young man, I must say. You only saw her this morning.

LAZULI: But think of all the years I lost before I saw her!

ALOËS (*aside*): That young man's a diplomat.

LAZULI: Now that happiness has come, let us lose no more time. (*Kisses Laoula: she releases herself*)

ALOËS (*aside*): It is almost time I interfered. (*Comes between them*) And pray, sir, who are you?

LAZULI: I? (*Bowing*) Lazuli, at your service. I pick up a kind of living by painting.

ALOËS: Portraits?

LAZULI (*unstrapping portfolio*): Portraits—landscapes—signboards—finger-posts—anything! Here are a few specimens. (*Showing them*)

LAOULA: How pretty! (Both girls, assisted by Lazuli, have their heads close together over the pictures examining them, with various exclamations of delight, when Tabasco, followed by Tapioca, enters L.3.E. Tabasco is furious.

TABASCO: Thunder and furies! Not at the palace! Why in the name of all the furies wasn't he at the palace?

TAPIOCA: I don't know, your Excellency.

TABASCO: Of course you don't! If there is ever anything you do know, tell me, so that I can—(*Sees Lazuli and the girls*) What do I see? The Princess and my daughter hobnobbing with a common painter! (*Going to them*) What's the meaning of this? (*Laoula and Aloës, seeing him for the first time, scream with fright and drop pictures*) So this is the way you follow my instructions not to go out? (*To Lazuli*) As for you, young man, I'll have you basitnadoed to slow music if I ever catch you speaking to my wife again! (*Drawing Laoula's arm through his*)

LAZULI: His wife?

LAOULA: But I am not—

TABASCO (*interrupting, aside*): Silence, Princess, in the sacred name of diplomacy! Would you ruin my mission and bring your royal father's wrath upon us? Especially on me? We must retire at once! Tapioca!

TAPIOCA (*eagerly*): Yes, sir! (*Gives arm to Aloës, who exits with him into the inn L.I.E.*)

TABASCO: Come, my love. (*Starts to enter inn with Laoula*)

LAOULA (*aside, observing Lazuli, who is standing mournfully, his head sunk on his easel*): Poor fellow! How crushed he seems! My heart aches for him. (*Kisses her hand to Lazuli, then exit into inn with Tabasco*)

LAZULI: His wife! She's married then! And I was so sure of happiness! The sooner I go and drown myself the better. (*Exit gloomily L.R. Enter the whole Court, preceding the King*)

CHORUS.

Bring on our King,
   In a stately and solemn procession,
      Cheer him and clap,
         With three "Hips" and a crowning
         "Hooray!"
Loyally sing,
   To the time of our tramping progression,
      Here's many hap—
         Many happy returns of the day!
Hail to our Prince—
   He was born for some excellent reason
      When springtime burns
         Into bloom for the month of May;
And, ever since,
   We have wished, at this beautiful season,
      Happy returns,
         Many happy returns of the day!
Bring on our King, etc.

Enter King (in Palanquin)

SONG.—KING.
(adapted from the American version)

I'm a King in everything,
   I am glorious, great, and good;
And I sit my throne with a stiff backbone,
   As a first-class monarch should.
I can turn exceedingly stern,

But I can, when I like, be gay;
And I may unbend, with a lowly friend,
 In my condescending way!
Simple folk, who can't see a joke,
 I hang them up by the heels;
Then I twist a joint to explain the point,
 And I ask them how it feels?
Courtiers say this coaxing way
 Has a quicker effect than a frown;
There's a special style in my royal smile,
 When you see it upside down!
That is so, as you know!

CHORUS: He's a King in everything,
 He is glorious, great, and good;
And he sits his throne with a stiff backbone,
 As a first-class monarch should.
 He's a King with a capital K!

DANCE.

KING: Clear out, all of you! (*King comes down*) I never saw such a
state of unanimous contentment in my life. What's the good of
being an autocratic monarch if you haven't got even one subject
patriotic enough to turn traitor! (*To crowd*) Be off, I say! (*Exeunt
crowd*) It's the kind of thing that only happens to me! Some
kings have all the luck! I don't want much—only just a grumble,
a murmur from even the humblest of my subjects. It isn't much
to ask; I know countries where they don't do anything else; but
my confounded subjects are so ludicrously behind the times. You
see to-day is my birthday. Well, every birthday, we have a little
fête, and, as an extra turn, I give my subjects a moral lesson in an
amusing shape—in the form of a public execution. It's astonishing
how successful these executions are! Last year's one narrowly
escaped an encore. Even the victim, as he mounted the scaffold,
said he'd "never had such a day," and that he'd "like it to begin
all over again." But this year I don't know what we shall do. We
haven't a single criminal—not even a misdemeanant—to whom
we could give the disadvantage of the doubt. (*Calling*) Siroco! I
never like to begin the day without a chat with my astrologer. It

helps you to make your plans if you know beforehand what's going to happen to you. (*Calling*) Siroco! (*Siroco has entered during the above, and prostrated himself on the ground. The King does not see him, and in going towards observatory, when calling Siroco the second time, he stumbles over him*)

SIROCO: I am at your feet, Sire.

KING: Have you fried out my daily horoscope this morning?

SIROCO: It's not quite done, Sire. I had a few small orders for horoscopes from private parties, so I took the liberty—

KING: You did, eh? What do you mean by letting small horoscopes for private parties interfere with mine? Is the royal horoscope so unimportant that you can let it get stone cold, while you brew some petty tradesman on a tip on the price of pigs?

SIROCO: I will hurry on it, Sire.

KING: There will be a very low thermometrical area developed in your neighbourhood, if you don't.

SIROCO: But your Majesty will remember that you gave me permission to accept outside commissions, to supplement my income.

KING: So I did. If I remember rightly, your annual stipend is not exactly stupendous.

SIROCO: Its smallness is very large!

KING: What is the extent of your weekly drain on the royal treasury at present?

SIROCO: Fifteen shillings, Sire.

KING: Fifteen shillings, eh? I don't think that's enough!

SIROCO: Your Majesty is too kind!

KING: A fifteen-shilling devotion strikes me as hardly robust enough for a monarch to pin his faith to. I must raise your salary.

SIROCO: Your Majesty overwhelms me.

KING: Henceforth you shall draw sixteen—but mind, don't let yourself fall into extravagance and make me repent my liberality.

SIROCO: I shall winter on the Riviera.

KING: Besides, I have adopted a more reliable method of ensuring your fidelity; for, between ourselves, you are mentioned in the royal will.

SIROCO: How can I ever thank your Majesty?

KING: You've got a nice little clause all to yourself, which provides that in the extent of our royal demise you are to have—

SIROCO: Yes, Sire? (*Anxiously*)

KING: You are to have ten—let me see, was it ten?—No, I think I made it fifteen—

SIROCO (*falls on knees*): Oh, thanks, Sire!

KING: You are to have fifteen minutes for any last remarks you may feel called upon to make, and are then to be entombed in the royal sepulchre with me.

SIROCO (*astounded*): Oh, Sire!

KING: Never mind thanking me! There is a general tickled-to-death air about you that speaks for itself. And now that you're aware what the future has in store for you, and that we are not to be separated, even in death, perhaps when you interrogate the starts on my account, after this, you'll put a little more conscientiousness into your work. But, enough of this. I want you to find whether the starts are propitious for my union with the Princess Laoula.

SIROCO: Such a delicate commission will entail the most exhaustive research.

KING: I don't care if it entails the housemaid's knee, as long as you find out what I want to know.

SIROCO: What I meant was, Sire, that I feat my mechanical means are too limited to do justice to the matter. For ordinary skirmishing among the stars, our dioptrical telescope can be made to do; but for the intricate celestial gymnastics which your command necessitates, there will be an imperative need for a catatropical one, with convex lenses and a convoluted focus.

KING: If I had a vocabulary like that, I'd sell it and buy Consols.

SIROCO: Now if know of a splendid Herscehlian telescope—best made—with star-finder and rack adjustment.

KING: Well! tell them to send it along.

SIROCO: I fly, Sire. (*Aside*) Sixteen shillings! I shall be a spendthrift soon! (*Exit into house R.I.E.*)

KING: I must not let my fête-day drift into the commonplace. A victim must be found at any cost. (*Exit. Enter from Inn Tapioca, followed by Aloës, who is trying to soothe him*)

TAPIOCA: I can stand his temper no longer! Let us run away at once and get married.

ALOËS: Oh, I can't do that!

TAPIOCA: Why not? We're disguised, and nobody knows us—we shall never have such a chance again!

Duet.—Aloës and Tapioca.

TAPIOCA: Spring will bring
    Birds that sing,
        In a clamorous
        Concert amorous!
ALOËS: Coming forth
    From the north,
        Bitter biting gales
        Stop the nightingales!
TAPIOCA: In the gay
    Month of May,
        I'll reveal to you
        How I feel to you!
ALOËS: That's too soon,
    Wait till June;
        I'll confess to you,
        Saying "yes" to you!
BOTH: Days of spring that dawn deliciously
    Change to chilly rain, capriciously!
    Cupid, clad in a bow and quiver,
    Cannot stay in the cold and shiver.
    March is windy, April showery,
    May is cold as oft as flowery;
    When the summer is blue above,
    That's the time for a maid/man to love!
TAPIOCA: Poets sweet
    Still repeat
        Love, eternally,
        Blossoms vernally!
ALOËS: Love is lost
    When the frost,
        Off the snowy tree,
        Nips the poetry!
TAPIOCA: Can't we dream,
    By the stream,
        With its flattering
        Murmur chattering?
ALOËS: We shall get

Colds, my pet—
  Highly critical,
  Laryngitical!
Both: Lovers' walks, beginning pleasantly,
  End in influenza presently;
  Springtime's changeable suns and breezes
  Cause innumerable diseases!
  March is windy, April showery, etc.
Exeunt Tapioca and Aloës into Inn. Re-enter King.
King: There's a young man following me who has evidently
  something wrong with him. I hope to goodness it's a grievance
  against the Government. (*Enter Lazuli L.R. despondently, not
  seeing King*)
Lazuli: There's but one thing to do. I must forget her—and to do
  that, I must die. After all, what is death?
King: Quite right, young man. The sentiment does you credit.
Lazuli (*curtly*): Get out of the light!
King: (*aside*) Hullo! That's promising! (*Aloud*) I only wanted just
  to ask your opinion of the Government. Don't you think that
  existing—
Lazuli: Confound the Government!
King (*aside*): By Jove! this looks healthy! (*Aloud*) Look here, you
  know when you talk about the Government like that, you run
  the risk—
Lazuli: Look here! If you don't clear out, I'll punch your particularly
  ugly head.
King (*overjoyed*): Oh, this is simply gorgeous! You don't really mean it?
Lazuli: Don't I? You'll jolly soon find out! Take that! (*Spars up and
  hits King on chest*)
King (*delighted*): At last! A blow! Thank goodness! He might have
  played a bit lighter, but still—(*To Lazuli*) I can't tell you, my young
  friend, how infinitely obliged I am to you for the service you have
  done me.
Lazuli (*hitting him again*): You'd much better have held your tongue.
King (*still more delighted*): Two blows!
Lazuli (*astonished*): This fellow must be crazy!
King: Not a bit of it! Simply revelling in a gigantic jag of joy!—that's
  all. Perhaps you'd like to hit me again?
Lazuli: A dozen times if you like.

KING: No, I won't trespass on your kindness to that extent. Once more will do, especially if it's before witnesses. You don't mind one or two witnesses, do you?

LAZULI: I don't mind anything.

KING: That's right. (*Calling*) What ho, there! Everybody! (*Enter from R. and L. Omnes. Tabasco, Laoula, Aloës, and Tapioca appear on balcony of Inn L.H. Kedas enters with citizens, etc. All are on except Siroco*) (*To Lazuli*) Now then, you needn't be too emphatic, you know. Just a love-tap, so to speak, will do the business.

LAZULI (*losing patience*): You will have it, will you? All right! There you are! (*Punches King's head. Everybody is horrified*)

KING: Thanks. My friends, I have the pleasure to announce that the fête is at complete liberty to proceed. A victim has been found.

ALL: Long live King Ouf!

FINALE.
(The Music of the first part of this Finale is by E. Chabrier)

KING: Young man, you have dared to strike the King!

CHORUS: The wretch! He dared to strike the King!
    Lazuli, Laoula, Aloës. I/He dared to strike the King!

KING (*spoken*): I repeat—Young man, you have dared to strike the King!

{   LAZULI: Alas! I dared to strike the King!
{   CHORUS: The wretch! He dared to strike the King!

KING: You gave a blow to me, you know!
    Such an atrocious deed
    Requires that the doer shall bleed!
    So at once you are doomed to die!

LAZULI (*aside*): To die! 'Tis well; I'd rather die
    Than live with love gone by!

KING: My friends, you'll be glad when I say,
    That now you need not fear;
    For our festival day will be quite as gay
    As that last year!

(*very pleased and slightly mysterious*) Open your eyes!
    Now you will see how a criminal bravely dies!

CHORUS: Now we shall see how a criminal bravely dies!

KING: What ho! my varlets there!

Bring forth the torture-chair!
CHORUS: The chair, the chair, the chair, the chair!
LAZULI: A grim affair, that kind of chair,
KING: My good young friend, I do not care!

ENSEMBLE. MEN. WOMEN.

The chair! the chair!   Is a rare
As you will notice   Sort of chair!
presently   Is a rare chair!
Will pinch and tear—
ALL: And surely will treat you unpleasantly;
It will flay you and slay you unpleasantly!
The chair! the chair!

"THE CHAIR"—KING.

This chair, on a hasty view,
    From other chairs does not vary.
But I hope I may prove to you
    Its virtues are extraordinary!
There's nothing much to strike the eyes,
    But if you sit you down a minute,
Then you will own, with some surprise,
    That there is something novel in it!
        So take a seat,
        Pray take a seat,
        Do take a seat,
            To be polite to me,
        My dear young friend,
        My good young friend,
            And you will see what you will see!
CHORUS: So take a seat, etc.
KING: Observe me now—I touch a spring,
    And set a dozen knives in motion;
Of all the humour of the thing,
    You haven't yet the slightest notion!
For when I press my finger-tips,
    Two pretty arms will seize and spike you,

While razors cut you into chips;—
　　I hope you'll tell me how they strike you.
　　　So take a seat, etc.

CHORUS: So take a seat, etc.

(*At end of Chorus to second verse of King's song, Siroco enters in the greatest excitement from house R.I.E. Music continues piano in orchestra through following dialogue*)

SIROCO (*interrupting*): Stop! Stop!

KING: What's the matter?

SIROCO (*greatly excited*): Thank goodness, I am not too late! Oh, your Majesty! if you only knew!

KING: If I only knew what—what is it?

SIROCO: Just now, as I was perfecting your horoscope, I made a most startling discovery!

KING: Well, go on. What was it?

SIROCO: This young man's star and yours are identical.

KING: What?

SIROCO: Your lives depend upon each other.

KING: What do you mean?

SIROCO: I mean that should one of you die, the other—

KING: Well, well, go on! The other?

SIROCO: The other will die exactly twenty-four hours later!

KING: Great Caesar's ghost! And to think I came so near committing suicide in the second degree. I feel weak in the knees to think of it! (*Is about to sit on chair, but remembers in time*) Take that infernal thing away! (*Guards remove chair*) (*To Lazuli*) Young man, I've had a narrow escape. I mean, you've had a narrow escape!

SIROCO (*aside*): It strikes me there wasn't any very great width to my escape!

KING (*to Lazuli*): I pardon you. (*Crowd begins to murmur*) My friends, owing to circumstances over which I have no control, there will be no execution this year. (*Crowd again murmurs*) But we'll make next year's a double event.

CROWD: Ah!

KING: And now, young man, I mustn't lose sight of you. Until further notice our Post-office address will be the Palace!

KING: You'll find there's naught about me mean,
　　Bring forth the royal palanquin!

CHORUS: What on earth does it mean?

Why should he ride in the palanquin?
(*Attendants bring on the palanquin*)
Kɪɴɢ (*to Lazuli*): Pray take a seat,
　　Do take a seat,
　　Please take a seat,
　　　　You must be needing rest;
　　For I repeat,
　　Yes, I repeat
　　That I will treat
　　　　You as a guest!
Cʜᴏʀᴜs: Pray take the chair,
　　Do take the chair,
　　Please take the chair,
　　　　And do not make us wait;
　　For we declare,
　　Yes, we declare
　　We mean to bear
　　　　You home in state!
Lᴀᴢᴜʟɪ: It appears quite strange,
　　A complete quick change,
　　　　And I don't know the why or the how!
　　　　Ensemble.

A Note About the Author

Charles H. Brookfield (1857–1913), Ivan Caryll (1861–1921), and Helen Lenoir (1852–1913) were major contributors to nineteenth and twentieth century theater. Brookfield was an English playwright who grew up under the influence of his novelist mother and her notable friends. Meanwhile, Caryll was a Belgian composer who studied music at both the Liège Conservatoire and Paris Conservatoire. Lenoir was the Scottish wife of Richard D'Oyly Carte best known for her work with the D'Oyly Carte Opera Company. Together, these three talents would collaborate on the English opera, *The Lucky Star* which debuted in 1899.

A Note from the Publisher

Spanning many genres, from non-fiction essays to literature classics to children's books and lyric poetry, Mint Edition books showcase the master works of our time in a modern new package. The text is freshly typeset, is clean and easy to read, and features a new note about the author in each volume. Many books also include exclusive new introductory material. Every book boasts a striking new cover, which makes it as appropriate for collecting as it is for gift giving. Mint Edition books are only printed when a reader orders them, so natural resources are not wasted. We're proud that our books are never manufactured in excess and exist only in the exact quantity they need to be read and enjoyed.

bookfinity™

Discover more of your favorite classics with Bookfinity™.

- Track your reading with custom book lists.
- Get great book recommendations for your personalized Reader Type.
- Add reviews for your favorite books.
- AND MUCH MORE!

Visit **bookfinity.com** and take the fun Reader Type quiz to get started.

Enjoy our classic and modern companion pairings!

Classic & Modern

www.ingramcontent.com/pod-product-compliance
Lightning Source LLC
Chambersburg PA
CBHW020449030426
42337CB00014B/1465